GU00985817

TEACH ENGLISH ONLINE – A HOW TO

How to Get Started Teaching English Online At Little Cost and Fast

By

English Teacher Rick

Rick Frost

www.englishteachrick.com

rick@englishteachrick.com

TEACH ENGLISH ONLINE – A HOW TO

How to Get Started Teaching English Online At Little Cost and Fast

Contents

Introduction

Hello

You are thinking about teaching ESL online, good for you. I teach English online and for me, it is a lot of fun. I really enjoy talking with the students, helping them with projects, helping them learn, collecting a bit of money, and the freedom.

This book is a short "how to", nothing fancy, just things I've learned along the way that can help you get started quickly, without extra expense, and hopefully avoid some of the mistakes I made. Suggestions, observations, some hints to help you jump in, save some money, make some money, have some fun, and do some good.

You Can Do It

Yes You Can

You do not need a degree in ESL or Education to teach English online. I do not know a single online teacher that has a degree in ESL, I don't.

There are very few start-up expenses.

You do need a computer – desktop, laptop, tablet, or a smartphone.

You do need Internet access of some sort.

You do need to speak English, either as a native speaker or as a second language with a minimal accent. Many online teachers are not native speakers, they just have good pronunciation.

Got that covered? Then you are good to go.

Why ESL and Why Online

You got to do something, might as well do something fun.

Teaching English as a second language online is fun, which is a good reason to do it. For me personally, that is the big motivator, it is fun and you are helping people.

With online teaching, you can set your own schedule and select your location, which are great freedoms, and more reasons to do it. No office required, no fixed hours, you can teach where and when you want; as long as you have students.

If you are on the road traveling teaching ESL is a great way to make some money and still be free to travel. All you need is a device to connect to the Internet and you can run your classes. It doesn't matter where you are today or where you were yesterday. If you are home, working or not, and you have the free time, teaching online is a good way to make extra money.

If you search online you can find any number of people telling their stories of how they traveled around the world teaching English as they went. Great stories and probably some of them are even true.

Teaching online is a business you can start today with virtually no overhead, start-up costs, or delays. You can jump in and be started teaching sometimes within a day. There are very few businesses you can start without significant capital input or an extended startup time; online teaching is a great opportunity.

Don't Quit Your Day Job

Get Real

The online education industry is booming. Google it and you will find incredible amounts of money are being spent by companies and individuals for online education. The universities are providing online courses and degrees. There are hundreds of online schools in all parts of the world just for English. There are thousands of individuals teaching online. Best of all there is room for you; new students are flowing onto the Internet every day looking for teachers. One report I read, dated May 25, 2016, predicted online education will be a $252bn industry by 2020.

Sounds great doesn't it, but get real, you can start today but it does take time to build up momentum. It takes time to build up a group of students, and it takes time to get comfortable teaching.

Don't expect to make a lot of money fast. Like any business, you have to put in the time and work to build it. You will see some income from your very first class, and as students come to know you and like you, they will return and you will make more. If you have 10 - 20 regular students, you have a reasonable income. You can build a business but be realistic about it.

Still interested, I hope so; you can do this. Next, we will talk about what you need to get started.

What Do You Need to Get Started?

How do the tires meet the road?

My goal when I started was to get teaching with as little expenditure as I could, as fast as I could, and still provide a quality class experience so my students would return. My personal rule of thumb – KISS – keep it simple stupid.

There are basically two ways to go about starting up your ESL online business. The first way is to work with an existing online company, an online school, becoming one of their teachers; undoubtedly one of many. The second way is to create your own online presence and draw in students. There are pros and cons for both approaches and we will talk more about each later.

Either approach requires that you have Internet access, which is your first requirement. There are numerous options for getting online so use what you have. If nothing else, go to your local Starbucks, if there is one, or a free wi-fi zone to connect. You will be giving up control both of your teaching environment and your connection, but hey if it works go for it. My recommendation is, if you are going to working from home and can afford it, get a DSL or cable connection. You do not need a lot of bandwidth, but the more the better. If you are traveling or cannot afford DSL use what you can find.

Secondly, you need a device to use with your Internet connection. I tried starting with an older 32-bit desktop system. That did not work out well for a number of reasons, mainly because of software incompatibilities. I then went out and bought a used 64-bit laptop with Windows 8.1 installed. Lots of people hate 8.1 but I've had no issues with it on this laptop. I have not tried it but I know teachers that use their smartphone to deliver classes. Whatever gets you onto the Internet will work as long as you can run Skype. We will talk about Skype further on.

My suggestion is to use what you have if you can. A new computer is not a necessary expense and there is always a learning curve with new hardware that may delay you getting started. You don't have to wait for a DSL if you don't have one, whatever you have to get online with now will be good enough to get started with.

Get started, don't wait, and do not put up roadblocks for yourself. Use what you have if you can and get started. Don't spend money you do not need to, you can improve things as you go.

Many students will connect with you using their smartphone, without video, but still, it is preferable to provide video if you can. Most online schools will require that you have video capability and will test it. Depending on your device you may need to get a camera and a microphone, but many devices have them built in.

Cameras and microphones are almost all now USB connections. Depending on your device the number of USB connections may be a problem. My laptop has only two USB connections; I have four USB devices to connect. My solution was a USB hub; I can connect four devices into it, and it into the laptop. Works great. The camera, microphone, and USB hub together where less than 30 bucks so not a major expense. A separate camera and microphone give a much more professional appearance to your classes on video. I do not like wearing a headset so I also use external speakers.

The used laptop was $150 and I already had DSL, so I was up and running for less than $200. Not bad for starting a new business.

Internet, computer, audio, video that is about it, you are ready to go.

Where Are You Going to Teach

It is a big, big world

I don't mean are you going to sit on your living room couch and teach, hit the coffee shop, or set up an office, I mean what part of the world are you going to teach in? Depending on your schedule and where you live this is a major decision.

Most students are of course not in English speaking countries, they are in China, Japan, South East Asia, Russia, Eastern Europe, South America, and Africa. If you have experience with any of these areas and are comfortable with them, then students from that area will be easier for you to work with.

Think of time zones. If you live in the US and want to teach in China, (isn't the Internet amazing), you can do it but think about the time difference. Most of your students will either be business people or actual school students and their days are occupied. They will be looking for lessons in the evenings mostly or early morning. The time difference between Beijing and New York is 13 hours.

10

What will your schedule and personal life accommodate? If you are a nighthawk or an early morning person it will make a difference where you want to provide lessons. Don't think you can jump out of bed at 3 AM and teach, it is not going to work. You need to be realistic about when you can be online. If you want to teach Japanese students and you are living in Tokyo you have a no-brainer, but if you are in Kansas then you need to think about it.

Ok, you have figured that out, next is the how.

Working for an Online School

Going with the Establishment, taking the easy way.

So you have your connection, device, audio, video, and you know where you want to teach. What next? You need to decide if you want to go it alone, create your own online presence and draw in students, or go with an existing online school.

The fastest way to get students and to get some money coming in is to go with an existing school. They have an online presence, an advertising budget, and hopefully students; hitch your wagon to their star and go. Research the area you want to work in, see what schools are available, and how they work. There are a lot of variations on how these schools operate and what they will require from you to share their students.

Generally and there are lots of exceptions, they will have a list of technical requirements. Often, they will have a minimum Internet connection speed. They may ask you to do an online speed test and send the results. https://www.speedtest net is a good site for testing your connection speed. Your school of choice may require video and certainly audio. Most schools run on Skype and they will require you to install it; more about Skype later. They may also require, at least for the interviews, that you have a professional looking environment to teach from.

Most schools will have an interview process that checks both your quality of Internet connection, maybe the looks of your location, and if you have the kind of personality or presence they think will be successful. Some schools will have only a onetime interview, while other schools will have four or five talks with you. My thought is the more difficult the interview process the better quality of the school and, probably, the better experience and pay as a teacher.

Pay attention to how they pay. The Internet is still the wide west and there are lots and lots of scams. Read reviews and comments from existing teachers if you can find any. I know one situation where the school pays to a local manager who is tasked with distributing the money to the teachers. He does, but he also takes a little cut from each teacher and tells them it is just the exchange rate. The teachers have complained but nothing happens; so what can you do. Similarly, some schools will have various penalties they will deduct from your pay. They are not concerned if you get mad and quit as there are more teachers signing up, and the turnover of teachers is part of their cost savings plan. You quit and they do not pay you; money saved.

Also, check out how the school does the scheduling of classes; there are two basic formats. Some schools will require you to be online at specific hours and you sit there waiting for a student. You may have back to back classes with only 5 minutes in between or nothing, and you still have to sit and wait. Other schools will allow you to set your lesson times, when you are available, and students will pick a time you have open. There are lots of variations depending on the school and how much effort they have put into developing their backend process.

One school I worked for had a backend process I liked. It allowed me to set my own schedule, what hours I would teach for the next two weeks. If a student scheduled a lesson from me I would get an automatic email telling me of a scheduled class. Then 2 hours before the class I would get an automatic reminder. This school had put a lot of time and thought into their backend system, and it worked well, other schools may not so check it out.

Pay, hey that is what you are doing this for, right, it is a job. The pay rate is all over the place. Many schools have different pay rates for native speakers and non-native speakers, often as much as 50% or more difference. Some schools have bonuses, don't miss a class and you get a bonus. Enough students say something nice about you and you get a bonus. Some schools will pay by the hour, and some by the class. Also, your qualifications may make a difference. Some schools will pay more if you have any of the certifications like TESOL, TESL, TEFL, or a degree in ESL.

Class duration is another area with a lot of variation. For some schools, a class is 25 minutes, for some 30, and I have also seen 45 and 55 minutes. If you are being paid $5 a class, (yes, that is what you are looking at with many schools, if you are a native speaker) the length of the class makes a big difference in your overall pay.

The good news in all of this is you are not signing a contract. Shop around. Find a school that looks good to you and give it a try. If it doesn't work out tell them and try another one. You are a free agent. You are also gaining experience all the time, and that is valuable too. Do not be afraid to try and negotiate your own deal with a school, maybe you can get a higher pay rate. The worse they will do is say no, so give it a try.

Going it Alone

Where the money is if you can get it.

Of course, the real money in ESL online teaching is going it alone. When you are working for an online school $5 a class is often the going rate. Running your own program you can charge what you want and many teachers are in the $30 per hour range or more. Also, you can do multi-student classes and a variety of creative things to build your business and make more money.

Sounds good but it is a hard way to go, takes time and a lot of work, but it is your business so why not. Search the Internet and there are numerous people out there offering classes, videos, books, and start-up kits for building your own ESL business online. Seems there are a number of people who have transitioned from teaching ESL, to teaching how to build an ESL Internet business.

That is not what we are about here; I'm not going to tell you how to do an Internet business. I will give you an idea of some of the major things you need to do to get one going, but in a word, it is marketing.

First and foremost, if you are going to do your own online ESL business you need to learn to do marketing. You need a presence in the social media networks like Facebook, YouTube, Twitter, Instagram, Linkedin, Reddit, etc. A website is a near must, and you must develop some material for all of these, some content. The goal of all of this is not really to directly gather students, though certainly that is part of it, or to teach, (remember teaching) but rather to build an email list. Once you have the list you can directly solicit students, over and over and over.

Here is a simple overview of how it works using YouTube as an example. You create a YouTube video talking about teaching English online. You give your contact information if the viewer wants a lesson and you offer a free something on your website. The viewer goes to your website where you again offer lessons, and you ask for their email address to send them the freebie. If they sign up for a block of classes that is great. If not then you have their email address and you start sending mailings to them advertising classes. You repeat this process on multiple social networks and over time you will build up a mailing list and paying students. All of this takes time; this is not a fast start process.

There is a lot to learn and do for each step in this process. Successful YouTube sites require frequent videos, with useful information, to build a following and stay relevant. Same with the other social media networks, you have to work them. eBiz says in July 2017 Facebook had 1,500,000,000 unique monthly visitors, YouTube 1,499,000,000. For sure some of them were looking for English lessons.

Your website will need to be professional looking and also have some valuable content. You will also need a way for students to schedule classes and to pay you. All of this can be done; people are doing it every day, making good money, being their own boss, and having fun.

One caution, be careful offing free lessons. Your schedule will be filled by freebie students that do not have a credit card or will not convert to paying students. It is better to provide some quality information for free and follow up with email offers of classes, perhaps at a discount.

Class Materials

A bit of this, a bit of that.

Some online schools will provide materials for you to present to your students. They will provide things you can read together, role plays, drills, grammar guides, what have you, but other schools will not.

Regardless, you should spend time putting together teaching materials of your own. This is a value-add for your students, if you are teaching for a school or yourself, it will help your retention rate. If you are going solo this is something you must do. Do not expect to get by just chatting up your students and amazing them with your clever wit.

Fortunately for all of us, there is an absolute plethora of information, teaching materials, guides, grammar sites, and videos available on the Internet for free. The difficulty is not in finding material but in picking through it to find what you want to work with. Be careful with plagiarism, it is too easy to do on the Internet. That said there are mountains of material available for free without licensing restrictions. Usually, you are just looking for ideas anyway.

YouTube a question and you can see how a dozen other teachers answer it and put together your own. Take the time to write out your own material. If you have a website up, you can send your material to your students for free, and collect their email addresses for your mailing list. During a class, you can send it to your student as a free value-added and improve your retention rate.

Developing and providing your own material will make your presentations better, and make you appear more professional. This will help your retention rate. You want your students to come back, over and over, so you need to give them something more than clever chitchat.

Getting Paid

Money

Sure teaching online is fun and it is great to be helping people, but hey you still want to get paid. Whether you are teaching for an online school or going it alone you need a process for getting your money. This is work and the better experience you try to provide for your students the more work it is, you need to be compensated for it.

Some online schools will deposit directly to your bank account. Usually, they are looking to do that with local banks. If you are traveling or working for a company in another country this may not be an option.

Many schools use PayPal. PayPal works but there are hidden charges especially if you are converting from one currency to another. You will see a hit when you take your money out. There are also charges to the school for depositing the money into your account, check who pays for that.

If you are flying solo using PayPal allows your students to pay upfront for their lessons. You will have to develop a system for tracking who has paid. If students are paying for each class as they go, there will be a delay while the payments are processed and credited to you. It works better if you can have the student prepay for a block of classes, then they can schedule lessons on the fly.

If you go PayPal be careful setting up your account. Your PayPal account name has to exactly match the name of the bank account you will transfer the funds to. Middle names, middle initials, Jr, Senior all that stuff can become a major hassle; PayPal has your money but they cannot give it to you. Working through PayPal customer service to straighten out a problem can be challenging.

There are other options than PayPal, online banks for one. Again, if you are going to use one of these, watch for hidden fees, all these services are there to make a profit.

One more thing about PayPal, if you are an American, they do report back to the government for tax purposes. Check the PayPal site and see how this works and if they report to your home country. Even on the road, Americans have to pay taxes.

Niche

Home sweet home, the comfort zone.

As you read various articles and sites about teaching online you will repeatedly come across discussions about creating a niche, an area of specialization. The idea is that you need to differentiate yourself from the other teachers online. This is true if you are working for an online school or creating your own, you have to be specialized, and you have to offer something unique. You cannot be everything to everyone, the universal English teacher. We are all conversational English teachers, we all teach a bit of grammar; you need to find something that sets you apart if only a little.

Each student has a reason for wanting to improve or maintain their English. Many students are professionals who are required to use English. You may want to specialize in business English. I know one teacher who has developed materials focused on doctors; doctor's English. I've had several students who were preparing presentations and needed the English reviewed; there is another niche, presentations.

Whatever your interests or background can provide you a niche, and students with a similar interest will find you.

Do not underestimate the importance of your niche. There are two main reasons students come back. One is they like you, you have created a personal bond with them, they like you and that is great. The other main reason is that you share a common interest or you are fulfilling their need, the reason they are taking English lessons; that is a reflection of your niche.

Website

If you are going to go on your own at some point you will have to decide if you want to put up a website. Depending on whom you read or listen to online some people will tell you a website is a must, others will say you don't need one.

The vast majority of online teachers work for existing schools and they do not put up websites, YouTube channels, or much of anything else; they rely on the schools.

If you are solo I think you need a website. Websites require some work and maintenance, and there are some expenses, but there are also many benefits. Your first expense will be hosting, your little home on the Internet, sort of like your street address for the online world. You will need your website hosted so it can be found on the Internet. This is not a big expense but it is an expense.

You also need your website. You can build one yourself; it is not that hard, using free tools on the Internet, you can really do it yourself. If you can program, you can bang one out, and you already know all this stuff. For the rest of us, there is software like Weebly and services like Wordpress that let you build your site yourself, quickly with professional looking results. Alternately, you can have someone build you a website, again an expense.

There is little point in putting up a website if there is no content. I said this before; you need to develop interesting content to put on your site. You want people to return to your site so you need to keep it updated with new material and keep it relevant.

Ideally, you want to get an e-mail address from each person that visits your site. This allows you to build up a mailing list that you can use to advertise your classes. This really is a primary reason to have a website, to get the email addresses for your mailing list.

Depending on how much effort you want to put into your website almost everything you need to do can be automated on the website. Collection of email addresses, sending of emails, listing of classes, instructions on how to pay for them, and even scheduling of individual classes can all be done automatically from a well designed website. With everything automated, it leaves your time free so you can teach which is actually what you are trying to do.

Ok with all that said, here is a simple and practical step by step 'how to'. I am not endorsing any particular services or software; this is just an example of how you can easily and cheaply build yourself a website.

1. Pick your site name. Take some time, do a little research on how naming effects your site, and give it some thought as you are going to have to live with it for a long it. It is important also because this is in part how the search engines will prioritize you in the search listings. Do not rush out and buy your name off some internet naming site. Names are free and many of the hosting services will register your name for free. Remember that once you have your name and your site is set up, you can receive email at your site.

2. Pick a hosting service to host your site. Bluehost is a big hosting site and easy to use. If you sign up with them they will register your site name for free. It will cost about $100 for a three year hosting agreement. There are lots of hosting services.

3. Build your site. An easy way to build a site is Wordpress. It is free. If you go the Bluehost/Wordpress option there is a button at

your Bluehost login that will automatically install Wordpress on your site with one click. This can save you a lot of hassle. Install the Wordpress on your hosting service before you start working on your site and access your site through your hosting login. Wordpress will try and get you to upgrade everything and charge you for it, but their basic free implementation and templates can build a very professional look site, with lots of functionality, at no cost. Go with the free templates to start with, you can always upgrade later when you know more about what you are doing, and you will not lose any of your work.

4.   However you are doing it, you need to get your site onto your hosting service and activate it to make it accessible through the Internet.

It is important that you understand that just putting up a site is not going to get people to it. You have to come up in the search engine listings. Getting up in the listings is not easy. You need to do some research and see what is required to optimize your site for the search engines. This is called SEO – search engine optimization. There is lots of information available on the Internet for SEO. It is well worth your time to read up on SEO and get a basic understanding of how it all works before you start to build your site or even pick a name. Don't rush it only to find out later that you made a mistake in naming that will hurt your SEO.

It takes time to develop your site, and get it to appear well in the search engines, do not get discouraged. If you are going solo, your website will be worth the time and effort you put into it.

Social Networks

It is a small, small world.

There are many social networks available YouTube, Facebook, Google+, Instagram etc. These are great places to promote your English lessons and also to list your website. The more interconnection between your social networking and your website the better your SOE ratings will be and the higher in the search engine results you will appear.

Even if you are working through a school it is a good idea to make a presence on the social networks for yourself in association with your school. Check with your school first if you can use their name, they usually are happy to get more free advertisement. Then put up something like a YouTube video "xxx school English Teacher Marry ". Why do this? If a student is looking at your school they will likely do an Internet search on the school to check it out. While searching the school your name would come up and maybe that will direct the student to you. If the student has picked your school, they still have to pick a teacher and it might as well be you.

My suggestion is to put yourself out there on two or three of the social networks to tell people what you are doing and how to get in contact with you.

Remember your social network listings and your website need to be updated to keep them relevant and interesting.

For SOE YouTube is a major factor, perhaps the major factor. The search engines watch for traffic between YouTube and your website, the more traffic the better.

Skype

Whats a Skype and how do you cook it?

Either way you go, you will need a platform to work on with your students. Your platform software, like Skype, will allow you to talk to, hear, and preferably see your students. The most common software for this is Skype. Basic Skype is free and it works; that is a great combination.

Skype is also easy to learn to use. If you happen to have two devices you can go online with at the same time, create two Skype accounts and practice between the two.

With basic Skype, you can do audio and video with your students. You can chat and send files. There is also a function that splits your screen and allows your student to see a file on your desktop, or you one on theirs.

You can also do multi-user calls allowing you to develop group classes. There are some limits, audio maxes out at 25 connections, and video varies depending on the hardware platform.

There are other voice-over-IP conferencing programs out there that provide more functions and are more reliable than Skype. Zoom is an application that does everything Skype does and more. There are several unique bells and whistles that Zoom offers that are very useful for teaching. There is a personal Zoom that is free. For whatever reasons Zoom has not caught on as well as Skype. Skype is ubiquitous; everyone it seems has it and uses it.

One issue to be aware of with Skype is that when Microsoft bought Skype they stopped support for 32 bit Linux. If you are running an older Linux system you are going to have a problem.

Students

A very important part of your success.

For my planning, I break the students into five general groups mainly by age/profession. There is nothing hard and fast about this and it does not really represent the student's skill level, it is just a rough guide I use. I've had several young school-aged students who proficiency in English was amazing, native level, and of course the opposite also.

Young Students – pre-school and elementaryHere I will admit my prejudice, I do not really like working with young children. I will take them as students but it is not my preference, I find teaching young children exhausting. Many teachers love to work with children. If you are into puppets, children stories, and all of that there is a large demand for teachers in this area. Parents all around the world want their kids to learn English and the earlier the better. This is especially true in China. This can be a great niche for those who enjoy it.

School Age – Forth grade through high school

These kids are usually fun to work with. They are looking for grammar, pronunciation corrections, vocabulary, idioms, and to develop listening skills. If you came through the US school system, I did, and unless you majored in English, I did not, you will likely find that these students have a better grounding in English grammar than you do. If you are going to niche this group, best to brush up on your grammar.

College Level - I have not really had a lot of students from this group; I think they are probably too busy with classes to add more. When I do get a college student they are often working on a specific project and want help or a review of their work. Classes are often back to back or several classes over a couple of days, but once the project is done so is the student.

Professionals - By far the largest percentage of my students comes from this group. Either they have a presentation they are working on or they have to deal with foreign business contacts. Either way, they are usually under pressure and want to maximize the value of their lessons. This puts pressure on you the teacher to provide the help they are looking for. I have gotten several great thank you notes for working through a presentation with someone, but that seldom translates into a returning student. The other groups tend to change teachers often as they want to experience difference accents and speaking patterns. This group tends to come and go as business needs demand. There is retention with the professionals, provided they feel you are being professional, and that they are getting their money's worth, but lessons are infrequent.

Older Students – retired or far into their careers Again I have a lot of students from this group, and they are the easiest to work with. Their English is usually already well developed and fluent. What they want to do is have conversations and practice speaking and listening. You will usually need to correct a word here and there but with this group, you mainly just have a pleasant chat. Be sure you prepare something to chat about; it helps if you can find out their areas of interest beforehand. These students tend to change teachers frequently because they want to practice with different people and hear different accents.

Student Retention

You need them to come back.

As I said every student has a reason for taking an English lesson. They have a problem they are trying to solve. The better you can identify that problem and help them with it the greater your retention rate will be. Retention rate, to a large degree, is the name of the game if you are to make any money.

If you are working for an online school you will most likely see a number of students, but few repeats unless you are providing a niche they need, or you have made a personal connection with the student. Many of these students are practicing their English speaking and listening skills, not developing new skills. They want to participate in a conversation, practice speaking and listening, with different people. Often they have bought a block of class times and will try a different teacher with each lesson. The downside is few repeat students, the upside is more students.

Another common situation is a student with a specific project. These students have a deadline coming up and they want help quickly. They select a teacher who looks like they can help with the project. This may give you several classes with this student as you work through the project but afterward, they will not return.

If you are going it on your own your students will be more loyal. They have already gone through a selection process and chosen you to work with. Find out why they chose you and emphasize that in your classes. Give them the help they are looking for and they will return.

Expect your students to turn over constantly, they will come and go. You need to develop a stream of new students to replace the students that drop out. Your financial goals for teaching, your ability to attract new students, your retention rate, and your attrition rate need to come into balance.

You and Your Online Presence

How cool are you?

This is a very personal call on your part. How do you want to appear to your students? This is partly driven by the niche you have chosen to emphasize. Also, I include in this your set, the backdrop the students will see or maybe hear when they are working with you.

You may want to be cool and casual, maybe teach from a park, emphasize you are traveling etc, wear a tee shirt. This may well appeal to school age and college students. I expect that this approach would be less appealing to older and professional students.

I know teachers that teach in their pajamas. I know one guy that wears his pajama bottoms and puts on a shirt and sports coat. He sets at a desk so the students cannot tell.

Whatever is comfortable for you and allows you to relate to your students is good. If you can build rapport then they will come back.

For myself, I have made an office area. Bookcases with books, a few personal items, and items that relate to the home country of the student group I usually work with. Often a student will notice something on the bookcase and comment, which provides a subject for discussion and a closer relationship with the student.

I also always put on jeans, a dress shirt, and a tie. I don't do this to impress the students, but to remind myself that I am providing a service, I am being paid to teach, and I need to be professional about it.

About Schedules

Time, it is all about time.

Scheduling your classes and the procedure you use for scheduling can make or break your business. Each student you get and can retain is a victory; retention is, from the business perspective, your biggest goal. If you have scheduled to teach at a specific hour, and then do not show, you will likely lose your student.

If you are working for an existing school they will have some procedure in place for scheduling or have required hours. They will also have a penalty system if you miss a scheduled lesson. When you sign up to work for an online school carefully review their policies regarding missed classes. Some schools will fine you the price of the class, as they have to refund the student, some are more severe. Missed classes are a major problem for the schools and they will terminate you if you miss too many.

If you are going on your own the same applies, you do not want to lose a student because you forgot the lesson. You have to develop a system that works for you. A combination of selling blocks of classes, being prepaid on PayPal, and having the student email lesson requests works. It is a little cumbersome relying on email. It is a better procedure if you can schedule the next class while you are teaching with the student.

Whatever procedure you develop it is important that you are consistent with your schedule and reliable. Always remember the student is spending money and they expect professionalism in return.

Another aspect of your schedule relates to the location you want to teach in. As an example say you spent the summer knocking around Europe. You had a great experience in Greece so you want to teach students in that area. Now you are in the States with a seven hour plus time difference. Perhaps you can schedule your Greece classes from noon to 4:00 PM. What about the rest of your day? Where do your evening hours match the evening hours of a country where you could teach? Perhaps you find a school in that area and schedule classes from 6 PM to 10 PM for that country. You are on the Internet, it really doesn't matter what the difference is as long as you can provide classes at the time the students are free to take them.

There are no rules; nothing says you cannot have two profit streams coming in. You can have one cash flow from your Greece teaching, and one from your other area of choice. Work with your schedule and maximize your online hours.

Degrees and Certifications

What do you really need?

There is any number of two, four, and six year college degrees you can get for ESL. If you have this kind of certification, you can move into a much higher stratum of the industry than we are focused on and demand much higher payment.

There are also a number of specialized certifications you can get. Many ESL students are college level and looking to go overseas to school or applying for overseas jobs. They are often required to take a specific standardized English test and are looking for a teacher certified to teach for this exam. Again if you are a certified teacher for one or more of these standardized exams you can demand higher prices for your classes.

The acquiring of a degree or certification is particularly beneficial if you are setting up to go on your own. There are many online schools you can attend to train for these certifications and where you can take the tests.

Lastly, there are a number of high-end online schools that require either a degree in ESL or ESL test certifications to work with them. These schools pay much high rates than the schools we have been referring to in this discussion.

Step by Step Map to Get You Started

Here's how you do it quick and simple.

You have made it this far, congratulations, you must be thinking seriously about getting started with teaching online. Don't hesitate and don't put up roadblocks for yourself. Put together what you need and do it. Below is a simple plan if you want to follow it to get started now, or almost now. Depending on how you get online you could be up and teaching in one or two days, it is that easy.

1   Get your device, what you are going online with – desktop computer, laptop, tablet, or even a smartphone.
2   Work out how you are going to get online.
3   You will need audio for sure and almost certainly video so get those working.
4   Install Skype and test it, play with it a little and learn to use it.

You are ready to go.

5   Now think about and select the area you want to work in, then research online schools in that area.

6   Get in touch with one or more of them and jump through the hoops and get online with them.

Even if your plan is to go it alone, it makes sense to start with an existing school to gain experience and get a little cash coming in. While you are teaching, gaining experience, and meeting students through the online school, you can be working on your own materials. You can get your website set up, put up some YouTube videos, network with friends and relatives to pull in your own students. There are many hours in a day, you can work for the online school and still do your own development and lessons.

Thoughts on Teaching

Some dos and don'ts, and watch out 'fors'.

When you are working with a student it is very easy to get caught up in the chitchat. Usually, these are nice people, they are interesting, and they are interested in your story. You are chatting away and forget that you are supposed to be teaching English, and so does the student, until later. After the class they feel like they have wasted their time and money because you did not teach, they just paid to have a talk with someone. I have seen many post class reviews where students have complained the teacher did not teach, they just had a nice chitchat.

There are two basic skills that the student is trying to develop. One is listening and the other is speaking. Find out quickly which your student is interested in working on. A common complaint from students is that the teacher never shuts up, they just talk and talk. Don't fall in love with your own voice. As a rule of thumb, let the student talk, don't say anything unless it is a correction or a teaching point.

Low hanging fruit, watch out for this. One school I worked for had a policy that new teachers were paid less than experienced teachers. They had a cut off for this of a certain number of successful classes at which point you would go to full pay rate. They also charged students less for new teachers, the low hanging fruit. I didn't realize this when I signed up with the school. The first weekend I had twelve students, wow I was excited. My first weekend and I had twelve students, I was hopeful; I thought I was really onto something. After that, I was getting one or two lessons a week and I'm thinking "what the heck happened". I started reading through the website site and I realized my first weekend my rate had been fifty percent the going rate and I had booked all the bargain hunters.

Similarly, even the online schools have a limited number of students that will be shared by the teachers. The more teachers the fewer students you are likely to have. Often schools will just keep adding teachers with no upper limit, after all, they cost the school nothing unless there is a lesson. This may be great for the school, lots of teachers for students to choose from, but hard on the teachers. Try and find out what the student to teacher ratio is and if there is an upper limit to the number of teachers that will be signed up.

One more thought along this line. The online schools often will have two sets of charge and pay rates. Native English speakers will be paid more than someone from a non-English speaking country, even though their speaking level may be native. Filipinos are a good example, their English is often native quality but they will only be paid a fraction of what a native speaker will receive. The schools will charge much more for the native speaker than the non-native. I worked for one school where they charged five times more for a class from a native speaker than a qualified non-native speaker. They charged five times more, but I was paid only twice as much. The non-native teachers I knew all were getting many, many more students than I was.

Perhaps it goes without saying, but be as personable and friendly as you can. Do not be too formal, you need to build rapport with your students. At the same time, you need to be aware of cultural expectations of your students, especially older students. For example, we Americans are in general a pretty informal lot; we speak much the same to everyone. This kind of informality can be offensive to some people, especially older people from a culture where older people are held in special regard. Likewise, young students may be put off if you are too casual with them when they expect their teachers to maintain a certain distance. You need to be aware of the culture you are working with.

When you get a new student try and contact them at their Skype address or email and acknowledge the upcoming class. Ask if they have something specific they want to read or work on. The sooner you can start to build a personal relationship with your student the better your retention rate will be.

Classes have time restrictions, but if you do not have a class immediately following it is good to let the class run a little long. Students will notice and they will perceive it as you being interested in them and in teaching them. This helps build rapport.

Depending on where you are, I live in a remote rural area; make some contingency plans for when the unexpected happens. The rest of the story, about my first weekend as the low hanging fruit newbie teacher, is that minutes before my first class was to start there was an accident near my house. An overloaded truck went through and pulled down all the communication lines coming into the area where I was living. Cable, phone, and Internet cables where all pulled down for about a quarter of a kilometer. I was offline for four days. I missed my first twelve classes and was almost fired from the school I was just hired by. I had to send pictures of the accident, downed cables, and broken telephone poles; they were really nice about it once they realized I wasn't a total screw up. I laugh about it now, but I wasn't then. You never know what will happen so make what perpetrations you can.

Lastly, don't expect to 'click' with every student. There will be some students, no matter how hard you try, you just cannot connect with. You and they both are just waiting for the class to be over, it happens; live with it.

Goodbye

Thanks for reading

Thank you for reading my little book, I hope it helped you in some way. Perhaps you have decided to give online teaching a try, or perhaps you have decided this is not for you. Either way, I wish you the best of luck.

If you have any questions or suggestions feel free to email me.

If you want to reach me:

Email – rick@englishteachric.com

Website – www.englishteachric.com

YouTube – English Teacher Rick

Printed in Great Britain
by Amazon